AMERICAN
PARABLES

Wisconsin Poetry Series

Edited by Ronald Wallace and Sean Bishop

AMERICAN PARABLES

DANIEL KHALASTCHI

THE UNIVERSITY OF WISCONSIN PRESS

Publication of this book has been made possible, in part, through support from the Brittingham Trust.

The University of Wisconsin Press
728 State Street, Suite 443
Madison, Wisconsin 53706
uwpress.wisc.edu

Gray's Inn House, 127 Clerkenwell Road
London EC1R 5DB, United Kingdom
eurospanbookstore.com

Printed in the United States of America
This book may be available in a digital edition.

Library of Congress Cataloging-in-Publication Data

Names: Khalastchi, Daniel, 1980- author.
Title: American parables / Daniel Khalastchi.
Other titles: Wisconsin poetry series.
Description: Madison, Wisconsin : The University of
    Wisconsin Press, [2021] | Series: Wisconsin poetry series
Identifiers: LCCN 2021013931 | ISBN 9780299335748
    (paperback)
Subjects: LCGFT: Poetry.
Classification: LCC PS3611.H33 A83 2021 | DDC 811/.6—
    dc23
LC record available at https://lccn.loc.gov/2021013931

For Haley.
For Kate.

It can't happen here? My friends, it *is* happening here.
—Philip Roth, *The Plot Against America*

CONTENTS

PARTY
TO A
CRIME

WHEN ON THE SCALE OF HUMAN SUFFERING

SECESSIONAL IMPULSE

PARTY
TO A
CRIME

AMERICAN PARABLE

In the dream we tell the lawyers
their aggressive line of questioning

insults the feminine discrediting
of our gymnastic national debt. As

precedential evidence, we shoulder
activist meat graffiti and toss it

from a small parade route we preform
around the courtroom. There are adjustments

to be sorry for, but we are touched by
all the beatings and agree that what's

important is to save our admirable resolve
for the next disqualified paycheck. Doors open

to a character witness asking us to play
the scene we are here to call attention

to: I am the police; you the dark legs running
up beneath your skirt; and between us red

birds are welded to the windows, stationed
like pianos in a junkyard fragrance

advertisement. There is no room against
your breathing for the crowd to reenact its

natural reaction, so we wait to be
instructed. What is it we owe the light

house neighbor light-skinned in holiday
lights resurrecting this recurring seasonal

price? We ask for a mirror and a comb
inside a cabinet. For a mailman bailing

bills. For a boy with sweaters fed howl
in his mouth laying tongues on shoveled

thirst so we hear only presents.

LAID LAND

We fight about the hummus not
  because I ate the contents you

  were saving for a party but
because our undervalued sedent

democratic freedoms are at best
  a modern factory of dumpsters

  filled with ditch wood
filled with butane

in a room with one long
  lighter tethered back against

  a trigger holding out
to be depressed. *Click.* Here

inside this kitchen there's
  a sinking orange body fake

  radiant in view, collapsing on
our evenings like a hormonal

teenage egging. Every night
  we sight the same undoing—a fever

broken wet from sweating off
embezzled weather—still sickened

past November in this Middle
        Western wretch. My father is a Middle

        Eastern immigrant who shaves daily
to prevent the fabricated active threat

of location tracking lice from bringing
        shame upon our family. The anxiety

        to celebrate what little we have
left leaves us as every couple

twined together and alone. So
        we argue. We yell and

        stomp and scare the cat and
one of us pretends to sleep

folded on the couch. What this
        government can't give to us

        we never wanted anyway. Get
up, my river bandit. They can't

take us if we rise.

We walk out- side to mow my lawn, and that's when
I realize you are in another country. I remove the
mower, prime the long-dead engine, and as I cut
the folded grass in sad, staggered rows, I talk
to you about revisionist history and the perceived
doctoring of foreign documentary films. You say, *I am*
offended, and I say, *but* *you aren't even* *here.* There
isn't a response until some- time later, the
yard trimmed flat, graffiti on my back, a band of
neighborhood Girl Scouts holding metal bats and
spray cans telling me that this is their turf and
I need to find a wife. When I go back in-
side I see you waiting on a bicycle trying to
tell me a secret. You don't move as I
step closer, but as I step farther away there is
a shadow on your stomach that breaks like a
window from which we watch the escape of a
chef, lace tied to his face, no surcharge a
carrot-free present from the zoo. A city
appears. We are reasonable contractors except for
all the murder.

VISITING HOURS

To be inside the lush
    of life I climb alive a tree

        outside the guarded rise
           of hospital where you receive

your treatment. Attached against
    my back I have a crate of caff-

        einated soap and aging
           pediatric drinks you drink to sink

your sweating. The nurses
    tell the officers

        that I am not a safety
           concern but I am still

concerned for your bald return
    to safety. In my tree, I eat

        peaches from a shelter
           can I later use to plant

with hands around
      my mouth and yell

          political obscenities
              instead of finally crying. You have

youth and roaming cancer and I keep
      an articulate distance between

          allowing myself to think of that. At your
              last known apartment, the traffic throbs

a swan of ruffled rivalry and everyone forgets
      an election has occurred. If I admit

          to you that none of our shared reticules
              have parachutes that means

we've given up. Here at last
      is the tidal wave survival

          recital we use to prove
              there's music. You will accept

the invitation because
      there is no other way.

JURIDICAL BENCH OPERATION

Promotional posters at the homeless shelter say shelter
isn't needed because the end is here. We look
outside and agree that while it may not be the
end—red trees, bruised shade, a man dog- eating the face
of his neighbor—it certainly isn't the milkmaid
we're accustomed to. You take a cup of soup and
spread the slick condition of its inside contents down
your dress, over a sore you have near your
birthing canal. The doctors you have yet to see have
yet to assure you the discharge you've noticed isn't
something worth a wreath. There is a baking
competition being held to raise the funds, but
you spend the afternoon setting up photography
equipment in a room we grew up convinced was
a lexical gas chamber. When I knock
on the door you knock on the door. When you
knock on the door I have already knocked.

TRIGGER WARNING

When the school shooter arrives
on campus my colleagues

in the Division of Irrational Cross-
Cultural Debt-Inducing

Activism open their lunches
and count aloud

the calories. From the conference
room we're ferried to, I hear

the calm alarm of numbers littered out
in breaks and pauses, breath swimming

through the dry asbestos echo
of our walls like harbor barges

bargaining their steam into
the night. Thanks to our

impressionably thorough plastic threat
assessment training, we know the

next step is to secure some
confirmation that our janitor

has yet to ever fully leave
the premises—that his laziness

of color and his tongue of
folded other are not missing

or the reason we have panic
in the dorms. The consensus is that I

should be the one to try and find him
because I do not have children or a state

official wife. I think
it is because of my beard

and over-olive
skin tone, but at least they

never mention my father's homeland
or his holdings in the bank. In

the bathroom, minutes later, there is bleach
and calcification solvent and the low

broad neck of a kind dark man with
clean white headphones nodding off

to voice and bass. One of us is crying for
the news of our shared difference. The other

is unbuckled at the waist and not relieved.

FIRST GENERATION: *YOUR ESCAPE*

A thief in my belief the street
        was where the police

sent you. Your uncle with a spade
        brought you home and made

you lay beneath a kitchen light
        lit as from below to look

like bedpans. You had
        a photograph, two cigarettes, a water-

soaked T-shirt hurt against your
        bone-wrung body wired up and

hung to dry. After sleep the meat
        of morning came and beat your

jaw with acne. You were told to take
        your things—rake rings from off

your fingers—and be ready to bark
        dumbly through the dark, a fled shot

bought behind the cost of your dead
       father. The books I look at now all

have you broken parts and radial, an exodus
       arresting us a people on

the run. There were animals enameled
       in your pocket hot with

cornmeal. You were not a child but
       inside you was a file saying

you would lose
       your colon.

AUDIENCE HOLDING INDEX

On television we watch an anchorman unspool his
Windsor knot and cut off his arm with an electric
can opener. His cohost is screaming in orgasm with
the weathergirls, and one of the producers is
pointing the camera at a drawing he's made of the buxom
Russian flag. Everyone is red with sick and nobody
wants to read the teleprompter. I can't tell
my mother not to worry, but I also drive her
to the pharmacy to purchase the hemorrhoid cream
we'll use as antiseptic when the lights
go out. The streets sink gelatin molds into the breadth
of our hometown. There are dead birds in our shopping
bags and on the hoods of our minivans. Camera
crews leash to an intersection not filming the
storm. The storm is not a storm but boats in a
basement. The storm doesn't have to come. It is
already here.

OUR BED AND ITS POSITION

It is night
      on a mountain, and I am not

            asleep. I look at your closed eyes
                dug deep inside your dreaming, the fingernail

moon clipping light onto our bed, and position
      the shadow of my unextended arm

            to act as though the mouth of a bird
                is on the wall. There is enough height

biting your side of the mattress
      that you are not disturbed when I play

            its beak to feed and rustle lightly on
                your hair, a nest in arrest

of this ever-bright dark. After heavy blood
      loss and muscle de-compulsion I lay

            my left wrist across your hip like a gifted garden
                trowel. In the distance, men articulate

our prized united sickness with canned aluminum
compression and automatic

gunfire. Between the slaps and echoed crackling
you adjust your knotted posture tossed

in pageant or a war. My hand is not a bird still
flight away from you is nauseating. This election

rope and trees we can't drive all night to save.

AMERICAN PARABLE

The wings didn't have a
body or the body didn't

have wings or we were kids
with a butcher knife and four

angry parents and we listened
to rap music and beat on our

chests and took off our shirts
and looked at our chests and

bought serrated spoons and dug
at our chests and put the body

of the bird and the wings in-
side of our chests and stayed apart

long enough for one of us to be-
come septic. You wanted to give

me a fixed bird, a bird that flew level
and straight through the grill

of my Dodge, its beak in
its throat like our shared

ancestral auto-osmotic asphyxiation
chamber, no breath in the room when

the room is a street behind a never-
gone bar where we always found

them. What else it seems I
cannot do is fly to you without

my body. We dress ourselves an
intestinal cotillion: feathers from

ribs, a flagpole of rafters, a police and
his funeral for us to can't stop.

TWO-STATE SOLUTION

We sit at the Seder table and
       dissect a live tractor. Everyone

      has forks and wet black
tanning goggles and when I remove

the lubricated rear axel
      gasket our guests become un-

      comfortable with such bland
strategic threats of loose

secretarial violence. The
      desert in my lungs coughs

      bottles unwed and we rise
to become a bread-winning

mechanic. A rag, our
      mouths, we fire the engine and

      return to the table dressed
now having purchased more

land as a buffer. I am asked
        four questions of *where*

        is the freedom? A man stands
on the tractor; his steering in

pieces we bring him a fight.

UNSUCCESSFUL TEST LAUNCH
DURING EASTER PARADE

A thin white guard at   the juvenile detention   center walks
us back to the   barred gymnasium where   we incite
a surprise   party. Everyone is   holding the signs they
made detailing the   names and   projected new-age
cryptocurrency gains of   the facility's two   most recently
paid malpracticing   obedience officers while   you and I
are pressed into   leatherette pilot   costumes. Once
the girls stop   cheering and the boys find   new places to
place their   expressive relief, we   all climb inside a
damp cardboard   box with a microphone and   a body we
aren't sure we   can put back together. I   want to be
in a clothing store   littered with terrycloth   robes and
supportive wireless   radio controls, but   instead we become
night with   a river and   a microwaveable
barn owl. No one   is disturbed by   the smell of
the feathers, of   the bone-breached   tendons up thrown
in the heat. You say   *where is the engine*   *to take us away?* I
am holding   your purse. *Where*   *isn't the*
engine I   say, and the garden   sheers come and
comes also   the bleeding.

I DO NOT HAVE THE MARKET CORNERED ON FEELING ANGRY AND MISUSED

We can't make
            the suicide joke

            anymore because
he really sucked

gas. Stripped down
            to his pillbox, unlatched

            the appliance, got
off in a fit of well-

exercised breath, no sea
            in his mouth, no

            humid relief. The only
experiment I should like

tried at my own
            death is an annotated

            failure-rate index
of neural-network

sonar detection when
        presented with two

        boxes made entirely
out of what we say

when what we do
        says we are not ever able

        to need without certain
constitutional mistakes. This

is not a real experiment, but
        our friend is really

        dead and I hear his body
will be opened

by science. A wedding
        occurred and there was

        a hostess. I sat in that
pageant and drew not

a step, arrested—the office
        lamp I turn on turning off

        on its own.

TRIGGER WARNING

When the school shooter arrives
on campus I take my Asian foreign

language student over to my office
window and yell *he is on a golf course*

in red American accents just to buy
a little time. There are sirens

in the building and our phones
are trimmed with light. We pose

for a selfie near my dying discount
grocery calathea orbifolia as a way

to feel our bodies and to digitize
an alibi. Between the rounding

corners of our carouselled alarm
we talk about my sterile haircut

and why for him he ever came
here. In the turned over under of

a shuttered filing cabinet he shows
to me his car keys and a tidy ironed

boyfriend, takes my hand
and makes a pointer pointing

stutter in his chest. It is true that
we are culprits caught in ever-aging

bait. We hold staplers and business
cards, a cavalry of calves. If there

is to be a slaughter we know
where they want to find us.

THREAT OF WAR IN SPRING

Here, too, the   night is framed against   its own pregnant
jazz. There is   a music to this   sudden spring, a
tenor pulling itself   low-branched and in   style, throwing
from the lawn great   measures of growth. It   was nearly
85 degrees today and   everyone was wearing   green. This
is celebration: drinking   on roofs, a saint   from a country
not lucky in   faith, faithfully facing what   can only be
called our heroic   uncircumcised   release. I
had one cigarette at   work and still hold the   chicken
and spices we   purchased last January. There   is a lesson
in this   manual about the   benefits of
crowded familial   prosecution, but   perhaps that
math leads   only to wild   imperfection. To be
a thief in this   country brings a young   heart not even
to the newspaper. If   I could be your   telephone, I
would steal myself back   to a less favorable   party and
ring. Can you   imagine me ringing? My   body
alight? My   torso intoning? My   chest a bald cavity
of numbers and   names; my   name a bald
house so   stuck in its place?

LAST POEM BEFORE MARRIAGE

Inside our garden is a garden of weeds
green-feeding the land around and

between the Siberian kale we planted
to be a catalyst for cradling our vacant

disposable income. In the yeast of
July's rising, we watch from our

bedroom as rain brings height to all
credible bull thistle, bottle grass, ground

ivy thriving alive in a lie, a shuttle of
life, a choking of ties we can sympathize

with. When we finally stand with the
appropriate plan and prepurchased

refuse bags necessary to brand the
mistakes we've gestated at the nail-

gated entrance, you tell me you
are no longer comfortable using

polyethoxylated tallow amine for this
particular project, at least not while

the neighbors are watching. I want to pull
the earth clear for you, but I don't have

the muscle. I want to carry my past and
burry it next to the rabid Swiss chard

held captive by active bright Japanese
beetles, but that too requires strength

and a willingness to admit that my
pointed disappointments point back

to me with fault. I hold the chemicals
and tell you there is no other

way. You hold a match, a cordless
oscillating fan, and the wood from

my old box-spring that we agreed to sell
on Craigslist after tallying up who else

had slept on it. *There is always another
way* you say, and then we find

the bunnies, no mother, wet
socks in a hamper, huddled and

waiting to be eaten or fed.

WHEN ON THE SCALE OF HUMAN SUFFERING

RETURNING HOME FROM HAVING FAILED

There are only two of us and a picture
       of my father bound in live

      extension wire looking at
a beach. First you are in

the middle. Then I am in
      the middle. Then you are

      in the middle again
and I am spanking you

with the unsettling news
      that the man we saw

      at the Nazi Preservation
of Historical Accuracy

Museum was in fact our last gap-
      seated gubernatorial mechanic. He was

      dismissive and cold to our tacit advances, but to say
he had come away from the trial not

understanding his part in
        your bakery fire suggests

        a misappropriation of the
four things we learned

during our seminar on the use
        of serial terror as a way to

        disguise our own umbilical
attachments. I prepare for us

a plan to redistribute what loss
        can't seem to be recovered. We buy

        a waxing kit. Straws. You convince
me to return to the museum,

to unwrap my spray-
        painted quarter panels well around

        a lamppost, to knit a new foreskin cutting
nothing away. There is so much lubrication

on the steering column that when
        the mechanic sees us at the accident site he

      is astonishingly frank about the walled
financial promises disbursed

throughout the narrative
            of his own Semitic

      liquidation. *What do we save*
you say *when his glasses and*

hair won't give us back our
            labor? I want to answer

      here, poor kennel, the
metal won't hold, but instead

the three of us stand, wet heads
            in a circle, safe in the weather

      that comes as a flood.

We position the
ask everyone at
condom. You
electronic invitation that
resistance would
country in heat, but
set and the off-
the Valium-infused
all forgot what
over. It is
even at the
security advisor. I keep
to my camera and
my people
everyone does.

horse to look like a
the Seder to
argued while
this show of
demonstrate our
by the time the
market Viagra dis-
wine coolers, it
exactly our
quiet in the
trial of our home-
a prosthetic
ride into
go. No one

pharaoh then
take out a
designing the
procreative
love for a
table was
solved with
seems we
survival passed
mall, quiet
bound national
nose fixed
town saying *let*
believes me. Or

TRIGGER WARNING

When the school shooter arrives
on campus our elected state

officials look concerned on network
television. Heavy breaded wonder-

bagged in underleavened suits, these
red-grown men keep hemmed eyes

trained on tremor-centered cameras
caught and haughty in their pores. From

behind a drainage pipe long-running
through my truant office, I shovel feed the

livestream beaming coverage on my tele-
phone. In the dark, as instructed, I am white-

washed, finally—the light lit brightly
back, a screen screened-in to out my face

a face. I can bite through this banana
but it doesn't stop the shooting. Doesn't

stop the brute suite sleeping force of horse-
corralling officers from knocking up

my door. On the scale of human suffering
my father is an animated leporine

cadaver, a living Middle Eastern man dead
to his home furnishings. To the cops I say

it is not my fault that I do not speak
Arabic. I cannot help them in trans-

lation. This tragedy is mad at me, a meaning
I relate. I place a pin on my lapel and

mirror every talking head.

DEVIATION ON RETURNS

You purchased a
        Spider. A 19

        81 red Fiat
Spider that you

bought—brought
        home, waxed hot

        in the unlofted
soft-rot garage—the same

beige afternoon I
        first lost time to the

        second past lapse of
my recently bruised crude wisdom

tooth surgery. In
        that car you

        hid your immigrant
image, unsettled

a check paved deep
       in your savings

       to add a new crisis
and run off

the gun. Maybe in-
       surance ensured my

       mouth would be
served, sutured and

gauzed right-white
       and pretty—or maybe

       you hemorrhaged a weak
year's pay without asking

your wife to park
       the dark wheels heel-pitched

       in our driveway, a damage still
damned as you flit toward

retirement. The tires
       I tired of deep in that

              brief post tooth-loss
sleep tried to hold us well

in the middle of
              class. *Get away*

              I said when you
brought to me ice, brought

to me Arabic sliced-rice
              prayer. You slept on

              the BarcaLounger next
to me on the couch, the

garage, your
              car, your 1981 red

              Fiat Spider. It was
Passover. When I

opened my mouth
              two workless days

              later, all of my
friends lived

in gated
              communities. I forget

              their names—the streets
and the golf clubs, the

power train engine specs
              I never could

              clutch. Twenty-five
years have shook and

took with them your
              colon, your knees, your

              need to be
colonized for having left home. *Belief*

you have said
              is the grieving thief pulling damp

              leaves from the gutter. Guts
I never had any. You gave up

the car. It lives
              with my sister. The

night throws its
sand. We are handled

in airports. The band
in your speakers

speaks coarse of the country
that saved you, divesting

investments still leaving me
thinking you'd

have more to say.

AMERICAN PARABLE

Well before you got your sick-
ness, the alternative high school's

prom committee had already
elected to hold their festive pre-

revelatory dinner in the hospital's
remodeled cafeteria. Seeing that hot

white limousine double-parked in
front of the Emergency drop-

off entrance was its own scholastic
cancer. You made the joke that

if these young women knew
what this medicine could do

to keep their bodies so dry and
hairless, they might want

your diagnosis. I opened my suit-
case and showed you the dresses

we could wear to the reception
now that you had more a figure

and I bore less a beard. Holding the
yellow strapless chiffon against your

buckled chest, you said *we look pretty
when we are hurting.* There was

music in the hallway, the sound
of a nurse's shoes

swallowing linoleum.

CONGENITAL PERSUASION SPECTACLE

We dress in our best postsurgery
      prep used stationary masonry gowns

      and attend a government fundraiser
hoping to attract a doctor. Your insides

are swollen, worn out by a storm
      combing back through your guts

      like a lawn mower feasting on leaves
in the fall and I tag along—your service

mechanic—bagged to ensure we conduct
      a disturbance. I think we'll have better luck

      lugging our rust with unhuggable crutches but
you are tired, and spotting, and not in the mood

for my digestive attempts to dissolve the attentive
      embezzlement of the still now seductive re-

      productive rights we're meant to be fighting
for. With fear and a mirror we get past security

then sit in a ballroom balling our fists, bawling
            a howl so scrawled in the night that the band

        claps hands to sing an applause from a
representative chorus just to drown us

out. You hold up a sign saying *we are in*
            pain but because you're a woman nobody

        hears you. You show them your blood,
flood legs over shoulders, bleed more

from your jaw since you have been
            clenching. No doctors arrive but a dentist

        asks for your number and if our engagement
remains arrangingly optimistic. I am sorry

for man kind I cannot be any other these
            boys keep swinging are blind. According to

        the state medical licensing board, a periodontist
is a certified trained professional. No matter

how it's presented, when they take away
            choice to agree with their feed we can

        always refuse to eat it.

FIRST GENERATION: *YOUR WAR*

That night a white-sight woman
　　　　manned your station at least that

is how I build it. By morning, you were in
　　　　a rented bed, lowered on

the floor, pouring sweetened powdered
　　　　milk inside your instant coffee coughing

cracks along the kettle as it cancer-whined
　　　　through noon. This is when you heard it

first—a siren ironed long against
　　　　the hillside sliding home, late breakfast

and your breaking fast American new
　　　　girlfriend making you a soldiered mannequin

a boulder on two feet. Soaked in
　　　　sweat you stepped debt-foot betting this

could only be a drill. You didn't know
　　　　the language, or your shoe size, or

that west of you in vests of blue the Suez
        had tuned through itself

by forces come again to draw you
        out. A rifle and Chuck Taylors you

weren't tailored for a fight. It was
        Yom Kippur. You shouldn't have

been drinking. You hitchhiked to
        your base and stood facing for your sergeant

trying hard to grow a mustache to grow
        must not aches growing up to keep

from shaking so that you could tell
        your kids what they won't

ask you about war.

THIS INDIGENOUS TSURIS

For not handing money
to the man who says his wallet
is a swollen set of foreign
orange board game

currency, I develop
an ulcer. Deep weed in dark
lacing, I bleed raw unsweetened
birdseed from the whole

of my holed colon to a white-
bowled cathedral in an airport's
holiday bathroom. Here, the song
sung is hummed with statistic

ventilation—shoes rapped
on wet linoleum, the elected
ache of dehydrated patience
letting go to get

let in. I work this worry through
my body, red present in my
face, chest reaching for my
knees to mark a pressing

punctuation: I am thirty-
six. I am passing away
plied paper and chalk-tableted
antacids, and I am looking at

my telephone to read your crude
obituary. In this publicized
facility, there is so much troubled
coughing it's as if your modern

illness is still thrilled to be
between us. This is the engagement
ring I wrung out
of my bank account. You cannot

attend the wedding but if I make it
I will try.

TRIGGER WARNING

When the school shooter arrives
on campus I lower the airlift on my

university-provided ergonomically
correct office chair and sit cross-

legged beneath my desk imagining
the various ways this might be

covered in the news. If the shooter
is young and white, we can discuss

animated gaming theory and light-
hearted cyber bullying. If the shooter

is young and black, we can discuss
blind oppressive history and the system-

atic distrust of the untucked cathedral
so aggressively present in what we've come

to call rap music. If the shooter
is female, we can discuss my personal

belief that what we've done in-
side this country is ask the mail

carriers to carry out the marriages
we've beaten down and cratered

because we grew up too busy
simply lunging into debt. But if

the shooter is Middle Eastern, the
reporters will take a special interest

in my father. They will want to hear
me say *here is the forest we left for leveled*

malls, my voice cracking, my back
still sore from hunching low beneath

the desk where I trimmed my beard and
confirmed paperless billing and made

notes on my hand not to ever
eat the celery or hold up signs

saying *rubberized this government a new*
return to form at a protest rally or equestrian

show, whichever comes first.

WITH ME YOU ARE INVITING TROUBLE

The cabin stands naked so we join it
    together. From our bodies, we steal bored

        denim and wood ticks, crouching low
            on a porch floor, under lungs of young

lodge poles, under the overhang of
    somebody's long-dead father, under

        a bag of sprung water we use as a shower
            to dig out the mission of what weather

we left to lead us here. In the dark cast
    of our shadows, we keep close to the

        feces and shedded shred nest of a pack rat
            family that gambled against sure-

handled survival and lost to a shot whose casing felt
    hot when it fell on my sandal. I am told, pulled

        tight in your towel, your shoulders are not bent
            like a wine glass stickered in price tags

because *attempts at rescue only make it worse.* Here in
    the unelectric parish of American irrelevance, my

        grandmother is still a crude museum of
            tumors; my cousin, still divorced with

only one testicle; my friend, still surgically unheld
    by the hand of a man who hollowed her

        nose bone just to know that he could
            do it. We walk inside the cabin and there

isn't any furniture. You have a toothbrush
    and the night, a lamp of moon

        ascending. With me you are inviting
            trouble. We are taken from and

cornered just like everybody else.

AMERICAN PARABLE

You tie a worn leather belt
loose around my neck and

walk me doglike through
the supermarket handing out

pamphlets on the benefits of
justified redistricting

in areas maintained by low asset
value indexes. We don't get

many takers, but when the
sheriff arrives, and you are

given the opportunity to defend
your pediatric riot as dischargeable

debt relief, you leave me with
the excited produce manager and buy

everybody guns. Officially, we can't call it
a disturbance because there isn't

any blood—just you in a courtroom,
the bench full of feathers, a chicken

without any wings in your
lap. During the opening statement

you say *this is the story of our swollen national
progression* but no one can hear you

over all the screaming. A sound
is released in relief of what's left. *This*

isn't right I say, and you ask me to prove
it. I open my mouth and breathe you

a boat on land to be flooded.

OUR SHARED RELEVANT IRRELEVANCE, OR A BRIEF HISTORY OF LOVE

I

At 35, the cat brings us a mouse. On the threshold of our bedroom door she sits between the legs of a modern wooden chair, pushing her gift toward you and your flashlight like a recently bar-mitzvahed teenager paying for deodorant. It is late, or early, and the house is baked in its own congestion as I sweep the stiff rodent into a dustpan and bury it in the air of our recently mortgaged first front porch. Reentering the entryway, I look at the cat, at the space between the chair and the threshold of our bedroom door and announce what I understand to be a sudden, reverent truth: *there is no blood,* I say, *no evident defense of how we live—in part—together.* I stand in the darkness. The night hangs around the clouded light like cheap, aggressive bunting. In the morning, we will go to work.

II

At 30, I collapse a building. Take the whole built thing straight down on a Tuesday and leave a small series of postdated checks to help those in the wreckage come out on their feet. In the parking lot of a national tax-adjusting agency, I call my mother to tell her what I've rationally done. *If it's true,* she says, *what will we do with the earrings we bought her for Hanukkah?* A bearded man dressed as the Statue of Liberty stands slouched on the corner behind me, holding a spinning sign and the keys to a wood-paneled minivan. *I wanna know what love is,* I say. *Stop singing,* my mother says, *this is serious.*

III

At 31, I am told to grab the crowbar. We are on a ranch, a Wyoming summer, big bursts of burnt earth stretched long along the skyline, a casserole suited too big for its oven. His ribs are broken, thrown from a horse, five lines in his torso struck-rivered and split. In the rafters of a barn we were brought here to clear, a thin mother packrat makes herself an awareness, six babies attached to her belly for feed, drunk bags of live organs hung almost at play. When instructed again, we grab the metal letter and stand on a tool bench epoxied in feces. *Hit it in the face*, he says, and nobody moves. The night before, in a bar outside of Denver, I lifted a moped to the back of a trailer and got a free drink and a married woman's phone number. You pulled me away, drove me to a mattress store, an airport, back to a cabin to wake by this barn, the throb in my temples unfit for our job. *Hit it in the face*, he says again and we engage in several minutes of action and rest. When it's over, I take the six curled babies to an unopened gate and remove their sprung heads with the blade of a shovel. *This is ranch life*, we are told, and the two of us nod: *true*. In the next year, one of us will marry; another will divorce; another will be back at a bar, drowned ice in warm amber, swimming his body toward something we lost.

IV

At 32, I awake in a hotel room with your bridesmaid late for brunch. We are roped in California, a severed melon on the floor, the day branched and never leafing while I root for missing keys. Suffered in the light of your interfaith-less union, you call my telephone to tell me what it's like to be on time. Later that afternoon, sick in the back of an over-odored minivan, I listen as my father sells my failures to the crowd: *you danced alone for hours*, he says, *your jacket still your only date. I know*, I say, and ask to stop the car. *You need a partner*, my sister says, and I open wide the door. Outside, white hills stillbirth around us like a flagrant laundered line. *It's true*, I respond, *all of it*. My mother looks at her watch. We never talk about the ways in which I trailer-wrecked your wedding, or how I never bought a gift. Instead, I eat Thai food on a field of paper napkins for my dinner, go to sleep with someone's wallet on my chest like a hand.

V

At 33, I collapse another building. Don't bring the
whole thing down with any calculated purpose,
but hole the wide foundation thin and flood it
'til it drops. From my chair outside the graveyard,
I hear the axe of your lame structure stomach
nothing and react, then write to you a letter saying
ship the body home. Later, in a scrimmage of bone
and leather-branded whistle, you find yourself
sick in my laminated bathroom. Eleven blocks
from where we first began to misremember, I tell
you what I cannot do then do it 'til it's done. By
summer, my therapist asks why everything around
me is always now on fire. *If I told you the truth,* I
say, *you'd put away the water.*

VI

At 34, the apartment is locked and I watch the clock inside it. I am not drinking. Am recovered in medication. Am a long boat of arraignments, no water to waddle, no crew on the deck save me in my dock shoes. The doctor is calling and I answer by pharmaceutically responding to the questions she told me last session would be asked: *there is always a boyfriend,* I say; *there are jobs in the East; they leave me for leaving them low in a factory, an elevator we have been riding in heat. This will never change* I say, and there is some truth in the trust of my thrushing bald faith. The neighbor boy cries because his mother is shaving. The doctor says, now, I need another doctor. I open my eyes to the staples I use to keep what I keep kept from coming kept out, and when I can finally focus it's you.

VII

At 35, the cat brings us a mouse in the house
we bought to settle my tremors. Here, we make
together a garden, make color on walls, make
grow the refrigerator ripe shadows of pay-
ment. Here, it is you I find hot-fleshed in your
sheets, hair wrapped in a package of course
evaluated metrics, my drumming alarm singing
me your emergency. What ways I can't stomach
you leaving are plenty, what electric discrediting
I will not survive. In the kitchen, I watch the cat
bathe herself long in production, her foot in her
mouth, her mouth feet from your foot. Always
I've waited for such relevant proximity. For what
we brought down to build up here together. For
you and your ambulant heart to appear.

SECESSIONAL IMPULSE

AMERICAN PARABLE

My friend///is an accident///had one///
with his lover///went through///with the impact///
now there///is another///Another///

halved home///Another///shaved dog///
Another///cocked box///of cold sanitized///
trophies///survived///by a rivalry///

somebody///lost///The newspapers///
say///our news///is a fire///
a hostel///told not///to keep feeding///

the cops///green-eyed///in a field///
of bright sub-///urban cubicles///Bathed///
in filleted///arterial///cadence///

I drive///toward the light///and arrive///
at a hospital///broken///too late///
for full rate///validation///To the nurses///

I say///*we are locked///in a garden///
savaged///by frost///but lousy///
with rabbits*///To me///they say///

we are terrible///ships///no berth///
for our crew///or use///in the proof///
So I draw///the burst night///bound down///

on the water///a cradle///knife-sliced///
then gowned///to the sea///I point///
to a bird///slight bite in its gather///the dark's///

one spark///cheap caving///ovation///
we leave///the cathedral///to burn it all///
down///

AFFORDABLE CARE

Phyllis has a cast casting shadows
        on her face and it's hard now for her

        to understand what she can't
hear. *I want to stop stealing your file* I say

but these regents are children and my chiropractor
        has ordered me back to the therapist. I speak

        clearly and do not signify my reluctance
to part ways with the bachelor party that

partially drove me here, hard jobs in our
        pockets, a well-whitened limousine canning

        our bodies, a dancer blindfolded and passed
through the air like feathered hair lathering

this creamery of astronauts. Whatever I can
        fit inside the Samsonite suitcase I bought

        at the estate sale for the dishonorably dis-
charged I will bring to the Mexican family

playing in the park outside the hospital where
        I keep returning. I want to hide behind the

        hedges and watch as they make a parade of
the bath salts and fresh insulin needles, but

I am drawn to celebration, the children yelling
        presents, the parents watching me cover my body

        in whatever I can give. Poor Phyllis and her
face, always hoping for a change. I bring ice

chips and a rowing knife to keep away
        the doctors. If there is an insurance arcade

        playing in her wallet, we won't let them
not receive it.

TRIGGER WARNING

When the school shooter arrives
on campus our polyester marching

band sits parched within my office
over-offering their stadium of wetted

metal horns. There isn't room enough
to bankrupt our solidifying terror so

I elect to take the radio and strike
away for home. Wearing cover on

my legs the color slack of some slight
other, I walk whitely through a blue-black

taser swarm of gnats and shielded
officers offended by my crease. Re-

leased to trees a scattering of rattles
cattle-stops then shops an echo. There

is a body in the street hood heavy
eyes within it, and I cradle my tie

pitched to dead-red pointing at
my belt. The intermodal station is

the only birth of nation not strangled
behind earphones or ability

to drive. A man in his shared wheelchair
is telling for a doctor. A girl and her held

child hide in pockets for a walk. What
we can be aware of isn't anywhere that's

listening. This radio has no batteries. My
legs give out a river; this news music

is a dirge.

YOU RIDICULOUS PEOPLE

In late May sun this early
        afternoon has shaded

                too much whiskey for me
                    not to notice my response—

head swum forward, heat
        welting on my face, enough

                wrong medicine belted to
                    my insides that I smuggle it

in lengthwise this drunk assisted
        living. My fiancée on her

                bicycle doesn't know this
                    about me—that I wake behind

the night hoping never it is
        morning, hoping ever to be

                under the turmeric loss
                    of day. The worry I have is

salt-lung heavy, tumor-pulling
          at my sofa cushion breast-

                    bone respiratory depot for
                              some change. I cannot change

my body to be any swell of
          celebration. I am leavened

                    with that fable. With that
                              nerve of uninvention. I am

leaving leaning only out the
          window for her show, what

                    emergency the work she has
                              of always saving lives.

AN APT RAPTURE

It isn't dark outside, but   you can't see. You   tell me this
from a payphone, standing   by an irascible   animal
auctioneer, a bird   on your shoulder   that could take you
away. I tell you to   take off your eye-   patches, but you
say you aren't   wearing them. I   ask if you are sure and
you tell me the   story of the man and   the woman he
thought was a   man. About how   you met in a black
market breast-   imaging clinic. How   the nurses
didn't want to   take your picture. How   the man
watched your things   while you went   to the
commissary; how when   you came back not   everyone had
qualities. *Oh, I*   say, and then   ask about the
weather. *It's not that   there isn't any,* you   say, *it's just that
I am in a   shelter and I cannot   see.* For a long
time neither of us   speak. I hear the   exercise of your
voice lift and   retreat; you hear my   radio say *the
governor is   not being impeached.* If I   had to take a
guess, I would   say that what   happened next wasn't
because of the   infection, but it   certainly didn't
help—the auctioneer   whispering gas   prices into a
megaphone; the farmer   foreclosing himself   in a tube
sock. During the   interview, we   comport ourselves, for
the most part,   properly. You are missing   a
tooth but I have my   wallet. The   bird sleeping
between us has   brought you no baby.

INSTITUTIONAL CONCERN

A girl outside my office
        window stands electrically

        uncertain, holding a one-
winged duck and her baby not

crying because it has been
        pushed inside a cradled

        plastic bag. There isn't
much commotion—the

bus driver announcing the arrival
        of the doctor, the doctor getting

        sick then losing his
toupee. It isn't raining. It is

never now raining since I moved
        to marry and I tell this

        to the girl while covering her
chest with blood and feathers and

the duck's bald wing well-shaved
to the bone. We don't address

the bag or the state of our American
miseducation. The girl is in

heels. Under her dress
an umbrella contracts. Light shadows

of wolves trace hungry the grass.

THE SOCIAL PURPOSE

They travel in packs
this gaggle of girls,
a lag in the way
they carry their bags

and haggle the heat
for a break in hu-
midity. Wearing flat
black regalia they swim

the damp air, a swarm
of clean bees not
mating the sidewalk
but stalling my way

back home just
the same. It takes time
and no water to determine
these daughters are boards

in a house gone Greek
without travel, a Midwestern
bellow of body on
body, stacked spoons

on the hood of an unaching
station wagon. They row
ever closer, hair walled
to their shoulders, and ride

as a circle their face
to the sky. No wave
of flag or bird to
mention holds their

attention but still
there is flight—white
hovering stutter, the brother
of earned tax artillery

dollars lifts in the form
of an aerial camera
drone to take pictures
of this sabled sorority. I sweat

in my jeans, a fooled man
of summer, and consider
collapse and resettlement
purchase. Mosquitos

displace their virus
containers and must look
from above like loose
caravans of nothing. I walk

the congestion detoured
and accidental, a truck
on a highway, its driver
asleep, hives in the

cargo leaning
the median. A crash
is ahead. A symphonic
electorate. It will shut

down this city. It will
keep us indoors.

STORM DRIVES US AWAY

It is just red
and the sick
holding, the
designed seems
as the doctors
to lose
small and her
belt, the
your cotton
hosed through
abortion in
gurney and
the hostess in
family holds the
puts a note in
a roof designer. He
him and
the organ the
of our carpeted
smell of raw
to rap music. We

rainwater but
young restaurant
escape route we've
now less
remind us that
an organ. The
body is scaled
lean toes of your
tube-top like
your uterus, a
reverse. I lay
you take
your mouth. A
hand of another
my palm saying
adjusts the lights
you and
doctors have
bodies. There is
animal relief. We
are gowns of the street.

because of the knives
hostess you are
had professionally
generically effective
someone is here
hostess is not
against your
swelling gut piercing
a rental car
stylistically unpaved
you down on a
the hair of
nurse with no
nurse who
I planned to be
and I grab
the hostess and
cut from one
bass in the
are listening

THE VIOLENCE OF MISSING YOU

In a rolling kitchen
table chair I wheel
myself against the cracked

refrigerator door and
do not adjust
my glasses. I am

heavy with rusted iron
supplements and
poorly labeled sleep

aid, but in this lake
of misconstructed
activism I talk about

your absence to the cat
I've taken in. Studied by
the presence of an ever-

level winter, I feel rough
heat move hard across
my chest, thrush rising

from my open mouth
like wet white carpet
on the lawn after

a storm. I need water
and I say so to the cat
now lost in honest

privilege which I can't
interrupt. In the
chair I am still

breathing while your
mother signs the papers
for your adult contemporary

casket, child-sized and
weighted by an ambulance
of song.

TRIGGER WARNING

When the school shooter arrives
on campus I pack my bag of

pickled mangos and set off to find
my wife. She works with her black

wrist guard three pale buildings down
the hill, and as I step into the cross

street bent between our reeling
offices, the police raise my olive

arms with lights and loud fire
of exhaust. There is a jogger in a

truck bed filming this a scene un-
folding, and I think of my grand-

father dead and carried back to
milk. I comply with their direct-

ives and note what has been mis-
taken—me a sand man walking

broad aboard a salt crane
parkway, them a spray trained rifle

helmets rented for a cure. In my
home, I own a portion of a cat and

trim Nordic styled linens lined horrifically
in tune. The city builds community

gardens and the deer collapse in
dinner. I am the wrong man. Have

always been. Where else should they go
looking when my cooking smells so far?

FIRST GENERATION: *OUR ESCAPE*

We made off in a Midwest
        city making out with non-

believers. The pulley strings
        and levers of our holidays

were cleavers, white meat
        reading your braised meters

like dogs. Two children rimmed
        with glasses, we were plastic

asked and basketed away
        from your nativity because

your native enemy was inside
        our ash-borered tree. Grain-fed

without your language, we
        never ran from what you

run from and keep wanting
        to this day. Night lights inside

your stomach like a car lot
        looting borough and there isn't

still a colon to help you
        with the process. I type into

the internet your high school
        and find rubble. Your daughter

has the flu. We are sick
        with disappointment but

everyone is fine.

WE WEATHER OURSELVES

Your insides were bleeding.
You were home with your dog

on the floor near a telephone
that you couldn't work because

technology grew and you hid
in a forest. From a wet divided

highway we called you a taxi
and told the dispatcher the animal

was trained. You were driven
to a stop, driven to a hospital,

driven with fluids, then driven
back home. Later, on line for

a meatless preprepared entrée
in the dining exhibition of a

Swedish furniture superstore,
I said to the server *we have to sell*

back the bargain so others know
the danger. She had dairy in her

body. She stood open like the house
you built gowned on a mountain

crosscutting the sky one long
lulling slit like light breaking under

closed doors in the dark, us wanting
a shadow to prove there is life.

SAD FESTIVAL OF MILD DISRUPTION

You buckle me wet to a new used car that sits
outside a collapsing junkyard and after forty-two
nights a tree roots itself through my fixed right
arch, arcing past bone and tissue and the skinned
cloth of the vehicle's sagging raccooned interior
roof, pushing small holes to a weather system
I call *Georgia* but you call *Trevor.* It
is hard to argue with the actuary agent, with the boys
you send me wearing sweaters of teeth, thighs
hard and scoring our volleyed new serve. There
is a sink in my stomach and it looks, you
have said, like the closet of the wife of
the son of a president made from the leashes we
leased through the local animal shelter's early
onset in- cinerator's club. There in the heat we
are sailed to a dashboard. *These* *bodies,* I
say, and then it is summer.

TRIGGER WARNING

When the school shooter arrives
on campus she is a pony-tailed

suburbanette with a box cutter
in hand. Greeked in reek geeked

letters, she has come to cut the
burqas off her colleagues at the

gym, steamed heat a screen door
preening this her doxed un-grad-

uation. Like my other pampered
campus rubber bank-inflated

partners, I am notified about the
threat while reading in my office,

an offering to breed a band of
everyone stay put. Ignoring walls

and calling halls of triggering
alarm, I walk atop a coated

chalk-prop stage to save
the day. The recreation

center is brass glass out-
side its ceiling, and the police

reach me quickly with batons
and then a favor. I tell them this

is not for me—this ca-
reening meatless woman

and her knife—but there is now
a misunderstanding. The vault

taut guts get rotten when I teach
the room that I have not been

taught to respect the spectral
wreck of our collective record

fall. I look from most eye-foldings
like the man who should be holding

foals at gunpoint on the news. Is
it never who we think it is or do

we never think? If these women
fight back there is metal through

their lungs. If they leave without
their cover what don't they

always lose? Who gets to hide
the knife is just a game

until it isn't.

AMERICAN PARABLE

The bed says *there is a man*
in me and I say *there is a man*

in you or in me? The bed says
listen to the statement again, so

I take a minute to write it down
on the back of a price tag you

removed only after we agreed
the personal massager could be

functional in many other
ways. The pen I hold is red

or black or reddish black and
I study the words and realize

the bed—as you have often
suggested—is correct. I want

to look at the man in the bed, the man
in me now starched and arranged, but

the man and the bed are surrounded
by lasers and I am afraid of macular

degeneration. You've written
instructions that tell me firmly

to stand in the shower, a storm of
cold water positioned as systems to

weather until the wheat in my mouth
becomes ever less dry. The bed says

there is a man in me and I say *okay, there
is a man in you. There is a man in the man*

*in you and a bed in his back and his back
is a tarmac lifting nothing away.*

PEPTIC BABYLONIAN ULCER

It wasn't raining but
        it rained or   it was wet

        on the deck or   I was wet
on my face

face covered by
        mustache   a staff

        stuffed to my   nose bone
knowing my   children won't

know what I   chose to keep
        buried. It   was raining

        or   the sun was down or
my son sat bare-thighed   sighing

on a rust hell-shoveled   bench swing
        netted in   his hair three

        birds three   stones three
parts of a   Simcha I

never thought I   would cele-
        brate. The rate   I paid

for this party   gate
security outfit fit   in the

budget held   out for
          my daughter's   white

          sub-urban   wedding
but not for   the rabbi's dry

kosher-blessed   meal
          flown in from   a city sitting

          not near   an airport. In my
hand is a ring   a story in

circles   a circuit cut
          crude when   I pulled

          this family's   tree. I itch
the root where   an ostomy

bag soon will be   sewn
          a surgery   my American

          wife will work   me to recover. I can't
tell you   this history

because it   is no
          longer mine.

WHAT I HAVE TO OFFER

The police say we have to put away our tanks. You don't want to give in to authority, but after a few hours of unceremoniously ineffective protests, you hand over your P.O. box keys and let me have my way with your stock market portfolio. I know you well enough not to know whether you are serious in your admission of having used the disgruntled animal hide we found behind the office furniture to reanimate a potential conclusion to the murderous case currently gripping the state of our less-collected union. There is water between us and also the theory of applied circumventive portion control when studying the effects of what has long been labeled our labored national relief. *Inside the shower*, you say, *it is very difficult for me to tell which one of us is losing. Not everything has to be a game*, I say, and then you hand me my stomach beat hard by a belt. If the science were easy, what stands in the doorway wouldn't stand there at all. Both of us are dripping. Something cracks in the megaphone. *Detective*, I say, *this is what's left of the registered light.*

FIRST POEM AFTER MARRIAGE

Against the tree you tie me so
        that I can't see

        the graveyard. Because
we have no

rope or galvanized utility
        chain remaining from

        the wedding, you bind
my chest and thin

thoracic nerves to the rooted
        set of our wet

        yard with a badminton net
I purchased

during the recently inflated
        threat of government

        shutdown. The light left
leaning leased shadows

through the leaves casts
        my frame a static finger

in the knuckle
of the earth. Tight

nylon on my only
running organ grows to mark

the time between
the neighbors' screams and

what you're doing
with the shovel. When I try

to, I can hear the sound
of your slight breasts dressed

river-held in sports
bra, sod pulling dirt rock

forming us a hole. We
will not be buried here but official

records indicate
we agree not to oppose it. Our employers

disappoint us and you want to buy
a goat. Going forward this arrangement

is how we'll make it through.

ACKNOWLEDGMENTS

Thank you to the readers, staff members, and editors of the following journals in which some of these poems first appeared: *The Believer Logger, EAT Poetry, H_NGM_N,* and *The Iowa Review.*

A selection of these poems was released as an audio chapbook titled *With Me You Are Inviting Trouble,* produced by *EAT Poetry.*

The poems "Our Shared Relevant Irrelevance, or A Brief History of Love" and "Deviation on Returns" were commissioned by the Iowa City UNESCO City of Literature's MusicIC Festival and performed with the Solera Quartet in 2016 and 2019, respectively.

This book would not be possible without the generous time and support offered by the Hermitage Artist Retreat; the encouragement of Niki Neems and Marc Rahe; the guidance and kindness of James Galvin; and the continued inspiration drawn from my family, friends, and students: Mark Ari, Josh Balicki, Jenny and Phil Blumberg, Jericho Brown, Mary and Ed Conlow, Steven Conlow, Amber Dermont, Dave Kajganich, Jason Livingston, Stephen Lovely, Shirlee and Jim Marcovis, Amy Margoils, Sabrina Orah Mark, Erika Meitner, Sevy Perez, Kiki Petrosino, Doug Powell, Justin Schoen, Sean Ulman, and Vinnie Wilhelm.

For your belief in this book, thank you to Carmen Giménez Smith, Ron Wallace, Sean Bishop, Dennis Lloyd, and everyone at the University of Wisconsin Press.

To my parents: כל זה בגללכם.

And to Kate: there aren't enough words. I love you (and Bunny)—
"Wherever you're goin', I'm goin' your way."

"With Me You Are Inviting Trouble" interpolates a line from James Galvin's poem "Jet Stream."

"The Violence of Missing You" is for Jason Bradford.

"You Ridiculous People" is for Denis Johnson.

"Visiting Hours" and "This Indigenous Tsuris" are for Haley Naughton.

Show and Tell • Jim Daniels

Darkroom (B) • Jazzy Danziger

And Her Soul Out of Nothing (B) • Olena Kalytiak Davis

My Favorite Tyrants (B) • Joanne Diaz

Talking to Strangers (B) • Patricia Dobler

Alien Miss • Carlina Duan

The Golden Coin (4L) • Alan Feldman

Immortality (4L) • Alan Feldman

A Sail to Great Island (FP) • Alan Feldman

The Word We Used for It (B) • Max Garland

A Field Guide to the Heavens (B) • Frank X. Gaspar

The Royal Baker's Daughter (FP) • Barbara Goldberg

Fractures (FP) • Carlos Andrés Gómez

Gloss • Rebecca Hazelton

Funny (FP) • Jennifer Michael Hecht

Queen in Blue • Ambalila Hemsell

The Legend of Light (FP) • Bob Hicok

Sweet Ruin (B) • Tony Hoagland

Partially Excited States (FP) • Charles Hood

Ripe (FP) • Roy Jacobstein

Perigee (B) • Diane Kerr

American Parables (B) • Daniel Khalastchi

Saving the Young Men of Vienna (B) • David Kirby

Conditions of the Wounded • Anna Leigh Knowles

Ganbatte (FP) • Sarah Kortemeier

Falling Brick Kills Local Man (FP) • Mark Kraushaar

Last Seen (FP) • Jacqueline Jones LaMon

The Lightning That Strikes the Neighbors' House (FP) • Nick Lantz